Copyright © 2016 by GM

ICT World

Development, Failure of Computer & Smartphone Technologies

Author: Ghazi Mokammel Hossain

Co-authors: Md. Fazle Mubin, Md. Izhar Tahmid & Md. Fathe Mubin

Designer: Ghazi Mokammel Hossain

Publications Format: Amazon Kindle E-Book format, Amazon Createspace Paper back format

Edition No: First Edition, November, 2016

Publication From: USA

Version: International Version

Published by: GM Publishers, associated with Amazon Kindle Direct Publishing & Createspace

ISBN-13: 978-1540605399
ISBN-10: 1540605396 (The book has been assigned a CreateSpace ISBN)

Email address: gmpublishers04@gmail.com

GM Publishers
My Book My Life

Table of Contents

Internet Security Issues

Internet Connectivity

Social Networking of Corporate Giants

Big data

Success of Outsourcing

Chronology of Outsourcing Disasters

Introduction

ICT (Information & Communication Technology) world is rapidly developing and new technologies are introduced every day. Some conspiracies, technological and security related issues are also happening in this world. But the development of computer and smart phone technologies are very effectively going on as the modern world people are taking this development positively.

In this book, we tried to show the gradual development of computer and smartphone technologies. For that reason, we followed segmentation strategy to focus different types of computer and smartphone related technologies in the different segments. Cloud Computing, Big data, discussion of different types of smartphones OS are included in the book. We not only showed the development of the ICT world but failures and conspiracies related to the modern day technologies are also presented in this book. Success and failure of outsourcing, internet and social networking security issues, failures and lacking of internet connectivity etc. issues are very effectively presented with real life examples.

The goal of this book is to provide correct information about the gradual development and some major failures of ICT world. As various types of computer and smartphone related technologies are discussed in this book, thus we have been presented all of these in article or summery writing format. Because it's hard for anyone to write about all the technologies thoroughly in a small paperback type book. The strategy helped us to effectively write every issues in a short format and the reader of the book will also enjoy the writings as all the writings are short article or summery based and easy to read.

Computer Hardware

1.0 Magnetic Tape

This article is about Magnetic Tape. It is said that the technology can contain memory as large as terabytes and is a very cheap technology for storing data. The article was selected to discuss about magnetic tape working process. It was first used for storing memory from computers during the 1950's. This makes it very hard and time consuming to collect any data because to collect data it is needed to start from the beginning and then the memories have to be fast forwarded until the end is reached.

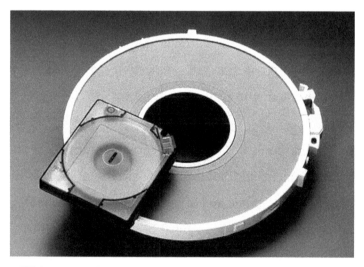

Figure: This type of Magnetic Tape storage was used in the early stage of computer development

This creates problems for the user to get instant memory. Recently, a modified magnetic tape has been invented by "Sony Corporation" which is said to be much more efficient than the previous versions.

1.1 Dynamic RAM (DRAM)

The article is on Dynamic RAM, author showed it was used to store bits of data and information in a circuit as an electrical charge. It was invented in the year 1966 mainly for the aim of Data Storage.

Figure: NorthStar 32K Dynamic RAM Board

As per some researches, the cost per bit of DRAM is relatively cheap too. And it was created in a very simple cell structure. DRAM is totally different than SRAM. The difference between DRAM and SRAM are given below:

Static RAMS	Dynamic RAMS
1) Static RAMS store each bit in an internal flip-flop which requires four to six transistors.	1) In DRAMS a data bit is stored as a charge or no charge on a tiny capacitor.
2) SRAMS require more power per bit and more bits cannot be stored as compared to DRAMS.	2) DRAMS require much less power per bit and many more bits can be stored in a given size chip.
3) The cost per bit storage is more.	3) The cost per bit storage is less.
4) No refreshing of stored bit is required.	4) Each stored bit must be refreshed every 2 to 8 ms because the charge stored on tiny capacitors tends to change due to leakage.

DRAM was modified over the years with aims to get rid of the drawbacks of it like data stored in it frequently needed refreshing. The manufacturing process was much complex, the data was considered volatile and many such reasons. As single transistor technology was used in the system, hence it was slow.

1.2 Small Computer System Interface (SCSI)

SCSI topic was chosen by the author because it is a popular bus communication services. Computers and peripheral devices are physically connected and data transfer takes place through a set of standards named Small Computer System Interface (SCSI). It's commonly found in Hard Disk Drives but can connect with other devices as well, despite all controllers cannot handle all devices. Specific commands are defined for specific peripheral device types.

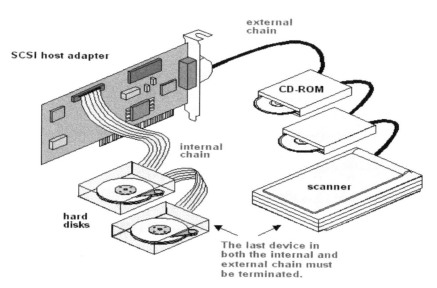

Figure: Small Computer System Interface (SCSI) working process

The history of SCSI depicts that it is derived from the "Shugart Associates System Interface" (SASI) which was of parallel interface and was disclosed publicly in 1981. SCSI was first introduced by the American National Standards Institute (ANSI) in the end of 1980's. Many companies helped and supported the SCSI standard industry. After its standardization SCSI has been used in many microsystems and pc server system. For its high performance workstation system SCSI is popular.

The main or basic reason to make this port system was to attach or connect devices like printers, hard disks, scanners, CD-ROM drives etc. The intention behind it was that it can have a faster transfer rate than its previous versions parallel data transfer interfaces. A set of American National Standards Institute (ANSI) that allows the personal computers to connect and communicate with peripheral hardware such as disk drive, CD-ROM drive, printers, etc. faster and easily than parallel data transfer interface is SCSI (Small Computer System Interface).

But one of the most important qualities of this interface system which is popularly known as "Skuzzy" is that it has backward compatibility. Thus, SCSI standards are backward compatible but all devices doesn't support all levels of SCSI. If an older peripheral device is added to a newer computer with a lateral standard then the older one will work at the older and slower data rate. In personal computers, instead of SCSI Universal Serial Bus (USB) is used but in server farms SCSI is still used for hard drive controllers.

Now up to 640 megabytes per second (Mbps) it can transfer the data. The transfer rate of this interface is about 640 mbps which was an instant success for ANSI and it became number one choice from that time and was used in many pc server system and micro-systems. Thus, the author have found it as a modern version that works with lower bit-rate in its older versions. From this discussion we learn about the bus communication namely SCSI.

1.3 SATA (ATA)

This article discusses about another type bus communication services. This article was taken because SERIAL ADVANCED TECHNOLOGY ATTACHMENT (SATA) is a commonly used computer bus interface at present. It has overcome the old parallel ATA (PATA) which is used to connect Host Bus Adapters to mass storage devices such as Hard Disk Drive.

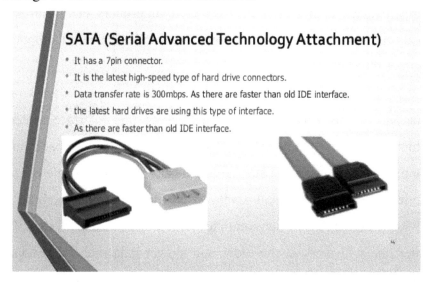

Figure: The features of Serial Advanced Technology Attachment (SATA)

It has several advantages over the PATA: reduced cable size and cost, etc. It communicates through a high-speed serial cable over two pairs of conductors and has replaced PATA in desktop, laptop and largely in new embedded applications. In 2008, 99% share in the PC desktop market was SATA's.

It supports hot plugging for which devices and motherboard have to meet the requirements. Advanced Host Controller Interface supports the advanced features of SATA on modern version of Microsoft Windows, Mac OS X, etc. And with the help of this article we come to know the attributes of SATA. ATA (SATA). PATA had a transfer rate of 133MB/s which is now replaced by a transfer rate of 150MB/s or 300MB/s by SATA.

SATA transmit data one bit per time which is also said as serial mode. PATA is said to be faster than SATA when the data transmission rate is compared using the same clock rate. In serial transmission if higher clock rate is given then it can be much faster than PATA. SATA uses one wire to transfer data so it faces less problem and gets higher transfer rate.

Standard transfer rate of serial ATA is 1500 MBps and 150 MBps is its effective clock rate which is also known as SATA-150. SATA II has a higher speed rate of 300 MBps. Few wires is used here. SATA port uses a seven-pin connector and seven-wire cable. It lets air to flow inside the PC case easily.

Operating System & Embedded OS

2.0 Android OS

The matter of discussion of this article is the OS of mobile phone. The article discusses on the Android OS. Moreover, this article was taken as Android is one of the most popular OS of mobile phones. This mobile operating system primarily designed for touchscreen mobile devices based on Linux Kernel and developed by Google is Android. It was first founded in 2003 to develop an advanced operating system for digital camera. Later, it was used smartphone operating system. Now it has further developed Android TV, Android Auto, Android Wear for televisions, cars and wrist watches respectively.

Android, an operating system primarily used in mobile phones is made based on Linux, developed by Android Inc. And purchased by Google in 2005. A green colored robot logo is its symbol. It is an open sourcing operating system. The OHA is a business alliance which helps to develop the open source operating system for mobile phones. The members of the Open Handset Alliances (OHA) such as Google, HTC, Del, Intel, Samsung, Motorola, etc. helped Android OS for its development.

Android OS contains many Java applications and java core libraries which runs under the java based object oriented application framework and the Dalvik Virtual Machine (VM). Android supports 2D and 3D graphics, common audio and video formats and carries

Google Chrome V8 Javascript runtime. Depending on the device, it supports multi-touch inputs.

Figure: Gradual development of Android OS

In 2008, Google introduced first Android OS in the name of "Astro". Few days' later updates named "Bender" and "Cupcakes" were introduced. This stepping into the market gained them huge popularity as well as profit. The basic reason was that it had a very nice appearance and very functional, efficient working system.

After 'Cupcakes' Google adopted the naming system of updates in alphabetic order of dessert and sweets, the latest being Marshmallow (6.0). Google play is one of the essential entries which is regarded as the official App market for Android.

Brands like Samsung, Sony, HTC, Huawei, LG, Gionee etc. are using Android as their OS.

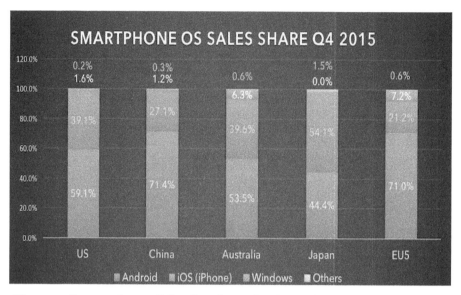

Figure: Smartphone OS sales share in the different countries of the world

Since 2013, Android has been the bestselling OS for Smartphone, tablets and also the largest installed base of all operating system. Over 50 billion Apps were downloaded in record of 2013. Between the technology companies, the success of Android OS has made it a target for flagrant action of the so called "Smartphone wars". And it is considered a big competitor of IPhone. Over a billion monthly user of apps of Android found in 2014.

This article helps us to know about Android and its different features. Thus, we analyzed the market of Android is on the rise.

2.1 iOS

This article is about another popularly used mobile phone OS. This article was chosen because iPhone is a widely used OS for mobile phones. IPhone operating system on Apple devices is known as iOS. We interact with iPhone's and iPad's through iOS which is the main operating system of Apple devices. After powering up the apple device iOS is the first thing shown.

Figure: iOS different versions gradual development

It also controls the setting menu by allowing to adjust the phone's hardware and features. It has an App Store to download apps and other things. iOS has already been ten years old and has been updating the software every year even quarterly if any issue occur. The updates add new features to make it better and improve OS.

iOS 9 is the latest version of Apple devices and like this every year they are competing well with the other mobile operating systems. Finally, through this analysis we can gain knowledge about iPhone and its uses.

2.2 Symbian OS

The analysis is about Symbian OS and its legacy. It analyzes the OS features and workability. Nokia had always been a massive influence on the mobile phone market since 2009. And the official OS used by the Nokia company was Symbian OS. Nokia started the Symbian in the low-end phones. It was the most popular OS in that low-end phone at that time. But after upgrading the Symbian OS Nokia had made it compatible for Smartphones as well.

Symbian OS was one of the top 10 mobile phone operating system of the world and an official property of Nokia. Other company had to take permission of Nokia before using the operating system. They became well known in the low-end mobile markets after Java. Symbian was the most used till some years ago. After upgrading the Symbian OS, Nokia made it capable of running in the smartphones and made it user friendly. Anyone could use it easily and it work efficiently.

Although the Symbian OS was very well designed and user friendly, its popularity was decreasing due to the rise of Android and iOS. ANNA and BELLE are the popular versions of Symbian OS which can be find in the Model-Nokia-E6 and Nokia-701 respectively.

Though, the smartphones were little less competitive in the market than android phones and iPhone. Still Symbian is used but its demand is getting lesser day by day.

OS vendor	Q4 2010 Shipments	% share	Q4 2009 Shipments	% share	Growth Q4'10/ Q4'09
Total	101.2	100.0%	53.7	100.0%	88.6%
Google*	33.3	32.9%	4.7	8.7%	615.1%
Nokia	31	30.6%	23.9	44.4%	30.0%
Apple	16.2	16.0%	8.7	16.3%	85.9%
RIM	14.6	14.4%	10.7	20.0%	36.0%
Microsoft	3.1	3.1%	3.9	7.2%	-20.3%
Others	3	2.9%	1.8	3.4%	64.8%

*Note: The Google numbers in this table relate to Android, as well as the OMS and Tapas platforms.
Source: Canalys estimates, Canalys 2011

Figure: The OS market share position of Symbian OS in 2009 & 2010

In Nokia's smartphones, the latest upgraded versions were Symbian ANNA and BELLE. In Nokia's dual sim phones Symbian OS was popularly chosen. Nokia C6-01, Nokia 700, Nokia 808, etc. phones are still running on Symbian Operating System. Due to the immense popularity of Android, iOS phones Symbian's demand is decreasing day by day. So we found once this OS was very popular for smartphone.

2.3 Linux Embedded OS

The article is on Linux embedded OS. The author discussed on Linux embedded operating system. The analysis identifies Linux embedded OS includes Etlinux, LOAF, LEM, Ulinux, Thin Linux etc. The major advantages of the Linux Embedded OS are: it is fully controllable, it has greater security and less chance of being breached, it is easy and simple to customize because of open kernel. It has been one of the most stable embedded OS and also that it can run on low end PC.

The author identified some minor drawback is the fact that it is a bit hard to learn how to control it and it is not the best user friendly OS. It is true that, Embedded operating system is not user friendly, because lots of features of the OS are totally unknown to its users.

2.4 QNX Embedded OS

The analysis is on QNX Embedded OS. The author said it's the most popular and user friendly embedded operating system. The discussion identifies QNX OS features and implementation. It is a well reputed and reliable operating system. The reason why it is so reliable is because it is a micro-kernel operating system. The most well-known of the QNX OS is the QNX Neutrino RTOS.

This OS has made a very strong and very significant impact on the Embedded OS market. It is a fully featured embedded OS which has the capability to scale down and meet up the requirements needed by the real-time embedded systems.

The article is very effective to know about QNX OS. And for this reason I selected it.

Cloud Computing

3.0 Microsoft's Azure: A Cloud Service Provider (CSP)

This analysis is about the description of a CSP. The article was taken as Azure is a cloud computing platform that gives a variety of services to form a cloud computing platform. It's proclaimed services till now are: Windows Azure, SQL Azure, Azure AppFabric and Dallas. Windows Azure is a service that allows to write code using the .NET environment. By putting the code in a Web Role or a Worker Role the work can be done without writing any applications.

Azure AppFabric is a gateway and works as a router between the items of Azure platform and the LAN dealing with authentications, certification and so on. Dallas, a place to buy and sell access to the services of Azure platform and is now a subject to be changed. So this analysis gives us an overview on the Azure CSP.

3.1 Engine Yard: A Major Cloud Service Provider (CSP)

The given article is about an important CSP. This discussion was done because it is popular and renowned CSP. In 2006 Engine yard was founded. It automates, configures and deploys application in the cloud as it is a platform as a service provider. It uses Java, Ruby on Rails, PHP and Node.js for cloud deployments.

They are independent and do not share their machines with others and for this reason they do not face any problem caused by other users. The applications are directly run by the infrastructure for example: Windows Azure. And for this reason users can run the apps at the time of platform outage. PostgreSQL and MySQL database are used by Engine Yard. For backup, AWS Simple Storage Service and AWS Elastic Book Store. This discussion helps us to learn about the features of the CSP called Engine Yard.

3.2 Atlantic.net: A Popular Cloud Service Provider (CSP)

This analysis discusses on Atlantic.net cloud service. We chose this CSP to know about this organization and their services as well. Atlantic.net is one of the leading cloud computing and hosting services. The main services provided by the company are Infrastructure as a Service (IaaS). Founded in Florida in 1994 as ICC Computers (Internet Connect Company Computers), it used to operate as ISP (Internet Service Provider) but later with the growth of the company, it became Atlantic.net and they started to provide co-location, cloud server hosting internationally as a cloud service provider, dedicated servers and managed server hosting.

It introduced cloud computing in the year 2010. The same year it added cloud computing API (Application Programing Interface). And expanded its business all over USA. We found one of its well-known clients is Orlando Magic.

Beside that it also act as a data centre for VoIP (Voice over Internet Protocol) system.

3.3 Rackspace: A Cloud Computing Platform

Rackspace is a large hosting provider. In the past they had suffered their share of data centre problem and now they are successful with plenty of happy customers with them. As like Google, Facebook, and Microsoft, Rackspace is also a hyper scale provider but not the biggest. The biggest is AWS. Around the globe they have many data centers which are managed by an army of engineers, system admins and operators.

In the world of cloud computing, all popular providers give instant access, customer care-service and utility-style bills and Rackspace clearly gives those benefits and to make it loud and clear that they have a strong market department. Rackspace and other big players of cloud computing use Openstack apps within their data centres. But Rackspace kicked off the Openstack cloud management platform project. It was said in the early days that Openstack is a young project and has a lot to develop. It was time savers for the coders.

3.4 VPS NET

The VPS NET is a recently very popular Cloud Service Provider which helps for hosting websites and gives very good services to it's clients. The service that VPS provides its users is a very good planning system which is very beneficial and also very easy to apply.

It also gives a huge amount of storage with a very cheap price range. One can even upgrade their plans which only needs a call to them. The clients who will find most beneficial are those who use a great amount of traffic or use a decent threaded software system. The customers are also able to host unlimited software sites adequately. VPS is also one of the most stable and adaptable hosting industry making it all the more attractive to the customers.

3.5 CloudSigma Ltd

This article discusses on CloudSigma Ltd, it is an Infrastructure as a Service (IaaS) company from Zurich, Switzerland. We selected this company to know about their services.

It has its cloud locations in Florida, California and even in Perth, Australia. It provides service on a utility computing basis. CloudSigma's virtualization platform is built on the Kernel-based Virtual Machine hypervisor built into the Linux operating system. They have developed custom hypervisor optimization ensuring maximum computing performance for virtual machine's running in our infrastructures.

Recently they have introduced a hybrid cloud offer through which customers can connect via its private connectivity to CloudSigma public cloud. We found CloudSigma has its customers and clients all over the world mostly because of its geographical presence and strategic expansion.

3.6 IDrive

This analysis is about a cloud based hosting service namely IDrive. IDrive is an online service for storage and backup with services which are very fast and user friendly which makes it capable of being chosen as an article. IDrive is one of the most reliable and fastest cloud file hosting service provider. It provides very good quality service to both the users of personal computers or a firm or institution with a large amount of computers.

They have modified their storage plan and made them available at a more affordable price. They are even offering unlimited storage facility at a much lower price than other cloud hosting service provider. Moreover, it has a well maintained and very flexible storage and backup system. And the file restoration process of IDrive is also a noteworthy feature of it since it is very easy and presented to the users in a very organize way. It offers a different plan depending on the size of the account but it is known to be very costly because at that same amount of price many other services gives unlimited space.

Adding to this, the file restoration process of IDrive is very easy and user friendly as the clients do not need to go through too much problem to retrieve their files. In short, it is a very good cloud service provider for those who have many computers and need a large space for storage and a very reliable backup system. So to sum it up, IDrive has a very easy, fast and also a very intuitive file hosting system though it has many limitations but still it provides very good service. And from this analysis we can know about the cloud hosting service known as IDrive.

3.7 Dropbox

The article here discusses on a cloud hosting service. It is a good article to chosen because Dropbox is one of the most easiest and graceful user friendly cloud file-hosting and storage service provider. It is an excellent service providers for personal usage but now it has also improved some of its feature which helps for users having many computers like the feature which allows two users to make change to their documents in the dropbox. And the changes made in the documents can be visible to the users as it is made.

It is bit expensive but dropbox provides very reliable and decent storage size for the users and it can be easily downloaded and used in almost all types of computer or mobile devices which makes it worth the while. This discussion helps us to know about the services that Dropbox provides us.

Advance Features of Dropbox:

The user can put any file in it, security system of dropbox is very reliable. Users can easily edit or restore any types of data, thus it is helpful for them to store and collect data. The company provides different types of data storing facility to its paid and non-paid users. Stored files are easily editable or downloadable from anywhere because the cloud supports all the popular smartphone's and computer's OS. User can share their files through dropbox and easily check the sharing history. We realized, the most unique feature of dropbox is file sync service, through this it can easily sync and store different types of files like, music, video, audio, document etc.

3.8 MegaCloud

The article determines MegaCloud, it is a popular cloud based collaboration service at present. We chose this to analyze it features, services etc. It provides various types facilities to its user. The user can use it cloud services through personal or enterprise account. Free user can use 8 GB storage of disk space and 8 GB backup storage.

The paid personal or enterprise user can use 100 GB and 200 GB storage to backup their data. The security of this cloud is outstanding; it can easily protect its data from hacking or worm attack.

We analyzed, the company offers high quality cloud based collaboration services at a reasonable price, and stored file can be easily accessible through Android, iOS or Windows based operating system. And the user can upload and download their files through official app from anywhere.

3.9 Crashplan: A Cloud Hosting Service Provider

Among many cloud hosting service providers Crashplan has earned much respect as a successful cloud hosting service provider.

But what sets it aside from other cloud hosting services is some of its unique features. One of them is the peer to peer backup system which allows to share some space for other users and which others can do for all of themselves.

The most astounding of its features is its reasonable price ranges which allow both personal computer users and also the users of several computers to store and backup their files. The backup system of Crashplan is also very reliable and easy to use which allows its users to get most of the control in backing up their files. In short, Crashplan is a very cheap and simplistic cloud hosting service provider.

DBMS & Various Computer Codes

4.0 Data Base Management System (DBMS)

The article analyzed DBMS structure. The topic was chosen to analyze Database Management System vendors and their services. It has recently played some significant roles. Oracle has been a well know DBMS vendor and known for the good quality of service that it provides. It has made some great changes to the DBMS strategy which helps the users more and the new strategy assists them to improve their financial condition.

Oracle has also upgraded their works recently which has got rid of the problems of the previous versions. The service it provides to its customers is reduced cost, easier storage, faster storage and many others too.

The discussion has great significant about Oracle's DBMS. So it can be said that Oracle is a perfect example regarding DBMS vendors and their provided services.

4.1 Implementation of MS Access in Data Base Management System

The discussion determines use of Microsoft Access in Database Management System (DBMS), it is a special type of service provided which has recently been considered very important application for data base management. We selected the journal because DBMS services has been playing many important roles recently and helping many companies with their work too. One of the most successful DBMS vendors is Microsoft. Microsoft has made many significant invention regarding DBMS.

Especially, Microsoft Access and Microsoft SQL are worth mentioning. The DBMS of Microsoft helps the customers to store and manage the databases and manages it much faster in an easier way. The analysis has provided remarkable explanation about DBMS and introduced DBMS of Microsoft and the features, services provide by the DBMS of Microsoft has also been added to the article nicely. The analysis shows the significance of Microsoft DBMS and the services it provides thoroughly.

4.2 UNICODE

This article is about the discussion of a character encoding standard.

The article was selected as it is a very commonly used character encoding standard and a very good example of character encoding standard as well.

0020	0 0030	@ 0040	P 0050	` 0060	p 0070	00A0	° 00B0	À 00C0	Ð 00D0	à 00E0	ð 00F0
! 0021	1 0031	A 0041	Q 0051	a 0061	q 0071	¡ 00A1	± 00B1	Á 00C1	Ñ 00D1	á 00E1	ñ 00F1
" 0022	2 0032	B 0042	R 0052	b 0062	r 0072	¢ 00A2	² 00B2	Â 00C2	Ò 00D2	â 00E2	ò 00F2
# 0023	3 0033	C 0043	S 0053	c 0063	s 0073	£ 00A3	³ 00B3	Ã 00C3	Ó 00D3	ã 00E3	ó 00F3
$ 0024	4 0034	D 0044	T 0054	d 0064	t 0074	¤ 00A4	´ 00B4	Ä 00C4	Ô 00D4	ä 00E4	ô 00F4
% 0025	5 0035	E 0045	U 0055	e 0065	u 0075	¥ 00A5	µ 00B5	Å 00C5	Õ 00D5	å 00E5	õ 00F5
& 0026	6 0036	F 0046	V 0056	f 0066	v 0076	¦ 00A6	¶ 00B6	Æ 00C6	Ö 00D6	æ 00E6	ö 00F6
' 0027	7 0037	G 0047	W 0057	g 0067	w 0077	§ 00A7	· 00B7	Ç 00C7	× 00D7	ç 00E7	÷ 00F7
(0028	8 0038	H 0048	X 0058	h 0068	x 0078	¨ 00A8	¸ 00B8	È 00C8	Ø 00D8	è 00E8	ø 00F8
) 0029	9 0039	I 0049	Y 0059	i 0069	y 0079	© 00A9	¹ 00B9	É 00C9	Ù 00D9	é 00E9	ù 00F9
* 002A	: 003A	J 004A	Z 005A	j 006A	z 007A	ª 00AA	º 00BA	Ê 00CA	Ú 00DA	ê 00EA	ú 00FA
+ 002B	; 003B	K 004B	[005B	k 006B	{ 007B	« 00AB	» 00BB	Ë 00CB	Û 00DB	ë 00EB	û 00FB
, 002C	< 003C	L 004C	\ 005C	l 006C	| 007C	¬ 00AC	¼ 00BC	Ì 00CC	Ü 00DC	ì 00EC	ü 00FC
- 002D	= 003D	M 004D	] 005D	m 006D	} 007D	- 00AD	½ 00BD	Í 00CD	Ý 00DD	í 00ED	ý 00FD
. 002E	> 003E	N 004E	^ 005E	n 006E	~ 007E	® 00AE	¾ 00BE	Î 00CE	Þ 00DE	î 00EE	þ 00FE
/ 002F	? 003F	O 004F	_ 005F	o 006F	007F	¯ 00AF	¿ 00BF	Ï 00CF	ß 00DF	ï 00EF	ÿ 00FF

Figure: The above characters can make you understand about the UNICODE

Unicode covers the all known language. Starting from all known human to even fictional scripts and all the way to modern language. Unicode is a system of setting up binary codes for the characters and texts. Officially known as the Unicode Worldwide Character Standard (UWCS), it is a modern idea of displaying, processing and interchange of written texts to binary codes.

The Diacritics is a big Unicode issue which is not familiar with the native English language. It represents the naked character of the Latin language, the pesky signs of the French acute, the German umlaut and even the Hebrew language. It also supports the Ligatures. Paragraph, paragraph breaking, line-breaking are also supported by UNICODE. It also supports column going top to bottom or bottom to top. Unicode encodes all types of language and so from article we learn about the main features of UNICODE.

4.3 NFS: A Text-based Application Layer Protocol of Red Hat Enterprise Linux 3

The article discussed on Network Filing System (NFS) of Red Hat Enterprise Linux 3 text based application. The article was selected to identify various types of text based applications. There are many text based applications many in the world at present and there are many new applications coming out also and they are trying to topple the previous versions.

The Network Filing System or NFS is a filing system where the file is mounted but it is covered in such a way that it seems that the file has been mounted locally rather than somewhere else. The users can use this system to centralize the servers which is actually needed. The author has provided excellent information about this text-based application layer protocols and also gave a good description regarding the applications and also the features and how this protocol systems actually work. And so the article was a proper one to be chosen to describe the features of NFS.

4.4 Freenet Service: A Text-based Application Layer Protocol

The article analyzes Freenet Service. It is a famous text-based protocol system and is used worldwide for the services it provides. We chose the topic to identify the new technology. Freenet is a service for the users that provides the networking service and many other required information. The freenet has many other objectives too which include efficient network services worldwide for the users for research and such other purposes.

It also helps the users to get reliable networking services, the users can get worldwide access to information related to research and other subjects. So the description of freenet has been given in the taken article vividly and so the author could provide the description of freenet further in the taken article.

The author has also given very good distinction on the objectives and the aims of freenet and how they aim to fulfil those objectives. And the features of freenet has also further been described in the article too.

4.5 UTF- 8 & 16

The most commonly used encoding are the UTF-8 and UTF-16. It can currently contain 120,000 distinct coded characters supported in 129 scripting language. The main reason it was developed was to overcome the limitations of other encoding systems like ISO 8859 which was widely used in many countries at that time.

Most encoding system had a lacking of using multilingual computer processing instead of bilingual computer language. We analyzed the recent UTF-8 uses one byte for any ASCII character, having same code value in both UTF-8 and ASCII. Whereas uses 4 bytes for other characters. The UTF-8 is one of the most popular 8-bit encoding form of Unicode.

At present, UTF-8 is the most commonly used encoding software the reason behind it is that it can encode all ASCII characters in a single byte but in addition to that it has also a backward compatibility which also does not take up much space and no space at all for the users of US ASCII. Not only for US and European users but it is actually the most space efficient encoding system for all users of different parts. And this is the reason why it is the most commonly used which is the fact that the US and the west Europeans are known to be the most amount of internet users around the world.

4.6 EBCDIC (Extended Binary Coded Decimal Interchange Code)

This analysis represents the discussion on a character encoding standard. And this article is a perfect example of the topic of discussion and so it was chosen. EBCDIC (Extended Binary Coded Decimal Interchange Code) is an IBM developed binary coding system. It can be used to write different characters in a binary system. The coding scheme of it is very similar to that of ASCII and it can be easily converted from one to the other.

Moreover with the help of EBCDIC a total of 2^8 characters which means 256 characters can be written with it which makes it an 8-bit encoding system. EBCDIC is a binary coding scheme. It's a method to transform binary number into character.

In early 1960's IBM adapted EBCDIC as a code for text files in IBM's operating system for its s/390 server and is continued to be used. It is used in larger computers in a file, each character is of 8-binary bit which allows to encode 256 possible character (letters of the alphabet, numerals, and special characters) can be possibly defined by the system. Though it is not widely used in personal computers but it is well recognized as an IBM code for minicomputers.

It comparably better than ASCII for the reason that it contains characters which is not in ASCII and also because it is a very compatible encoding system for small computers and thus more popular. Not only that but it is also popular internationally and also very widely used in personal computers.

This analysis helps us on learning the characteristics of EBCDIC. It was first coined by IBM and they made it to use for their large OS. It converts characters into binary numbers. This system is more widely used in mini-computers of IBM rather than the normal personal computers. We found this can be compared to ASCII system of encoding but ASCII can depict more characters than EBCDIC. Thus IBM's PC's and workstation OS uses ASCII instead of EBCDIC.

4.7 Amazon Web Service: An IoT Based System

The given article is about Amazon Web Service which is one of the biggest and famous companies. The author said it is a subject which is very popular at the moment and it is in trend at the moment. We selected the article to analyze internet of things working process and different software and other services.

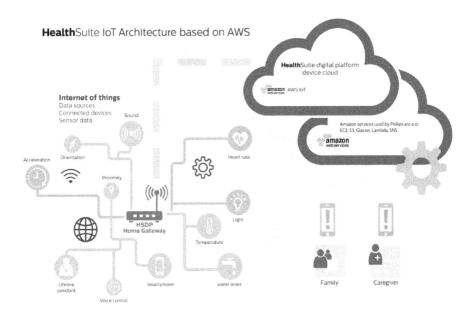

Figure: HealthSuite IoT Architecture based on AWS

It is a very successful and developing company which is doing a great job at providing good quality services. The services that it provides is mainly the storing of data and information. And so the services of amazon web services can be described as fluent as it gives good services related to data storage and at present has also done the same for smartphones too.

The analysis has given a good description of the services and the features of amazon web service. We know detailed information given in the article about the technology.

4.8 Google's IoT Deployment

The article discussed the major problems of Google's IoT deployment. We selected the article to identify Internet of Things (IoT) new and life changing services which has recently emerged. With this service we can control and monitor our environment from any place with the help of some technologies. The recent dive into internet of things has been made by Google.

Google has made a decision that they will star giving services and technologies to the users as a product of internet of things. This idea has proved a little costly for them because of some setbacks in their services and their technologies. The author has provided great description about the applications of internet of things that Google has provided and the reason of their downfall too. So the article was taken because of the distinct features mentioned in it. And for all these reasons the article was taken.

Internet Security Issues

5.0 Ransomware

It is a new type of internet security issue which has taken the internet by storm. This internet security issue was selected to identify the new internet security threat called Ransomware.

It is a type of malware from which different data and information of the targeted victim is fished out and then it is used to take ransom by blackmailing that information. It is a recent problem that has hit the internet world. It is basically hijacking of information bandwidth data so that it can later be used as a source of blackmail to want ransom from the victim.

One of these major incident is regarding the New York Times and BBC being attacked and this created great amount of problems for these major companies. Recently the New York Times and BBC were reported that a malicious malware was used to fake advertise, this process is called malvertise. And then this malvertisement was used to take advantage of the victim and then they were blackmailed and then the attacker demanded ransom for the information collected.

A very recent incident regarding Ransomware is the attack on the mac users. Recently some mac users have been facing the problem of being attacked by Ransomware. And so apple have been reviewing the problem and were quiet worried about this problem. The taken article is good example of the required subject and the author also gave a good description about the problem too. And so the taken article has greatly helped this work.

The author has given a good description too. The given article signifies a major incident regarding Ransomware as well.

5.1 Phishing: A Social Engineering Attack

This article is about one of the different types of social engineering attack. This article was taken as it is a common internet security breaching technique. Phishing is a very common method of scamming people with the impersonation of opening a business or also a call for recruitment to a business. This type of impersonation is the most common method of scamming people in the internet and the emails sent to people are all scams for people to give them their account details so that they can fraud them.

This is mostly seen in different ads on a website or even sent to email accounts of random people or sometimes some specific people. It is necessary that no one should send information about one's account because no company will ask to send these information through insecure methods. And so it should be taken in consideration to delete these emails and not to comply with their demands.

Phishing is a form of fraud where attackers try to get information about login credentials or account information by going in taking the form of a reputable entity or a person with email ID. The victim receives a message where there are malware links and traps the victim. Like this the password or ID of the victim goes to the attacker. Cybercriminals do this phishing as it is easy to lure people to click on a link than to break the defense of the computer. The emails are often built on the year's major event and also takes the advantage of the breaking news.

5.2 Pretexting: Major Social Engineering Attack

This article is about a common social engineering attack. This article is a very infamous example of this types of attack. An individual lies to obtain privileged data from another is known as pretexting. Pretexting is common online scamming scheme in which the attacker impersonates a totally different identity in order to get different information about a specific person or any person as targeted. These attackers will provide a solid pretext of their identity so that they can trick people to think of him as a different person and the gaining their information for their benefits.

This type of method can also be used in tricking people into jobs or services he/she has never done or provide before respectively. Pretexting is not only a frauding method in social engineering but it is also used in different sectors for both positive and also negative usage. So to refrain from this problem one must thoroughly check the information about the identity that the other party provides. With this false motive of the liar he pretends to take information of the person he is talking to. After knowing the person he asks some questions to gather key individual identifiers such as the social security number, mother's maiden name, etc.

Like this they access to the financial data of an individual. In 1999, it was banned by the GLB Act. The FTC has taken many steps and has filled several lawsuits against the online pretexters. They have recommended not to give personal information in the phones or over the internet unless you know the contactors. This article helps us to know about the different methods and techniques of getting attacked by Pretexting.

5.3 Social Engineering Attack in RSA

The article discusses on mysterious attack occurred in 2011 on the RSA company. I found it as a helpful example of social engineering attacks. What was known is that some information related to RSA's SecurID was somehow shifted hands as a result RSA's parent company had to pay $66 million. Though it is still a mystery what information was actually exposed but it was assumed, maybe the source code or the cryptographic seed values are plausible explanations. The attacker in this case sent two phishing emails to lower employees. The e-mail had an excel file attached to it named *"2011 Recruitment plan.xls"*.

The spreadsheet contained a zero day exploit which can install a backdoor though an Adobe Flash vulnerability. We examined it breached the security through social engineering. It is considered one of the top 5 high profile social engineering attack.

5.4 Most Famous Twitter Account Hack

This article discusses on the Twitter Account of Associate Press News wire service was hacked in 2013 by Syrian electronic army. We identified it as a helpful example of social engineering attacks.

The hackers then twitted a false tweet about explosions in White House and that the President Barack Obama is injured. The tweet looked so authentic that within a minute DOW (Major Stock Exchange of US) started the nosedive and dropped 150 points.

Figure: This tweet of the Syrian electronic army through the hacked account of AP had been created awkward moment in the entire world

It took only 2 minute to disclose that it was an erroneous tweet. But within this 2 minutes, massive damage was done. This attack was also started by phishing message. The attacker sent a phishing message to an AP's employee which lack the sender's name, but other than that it looked really authentic enough to fool anyone. Thus, we realized this attack was also a result of social engineering attack.

5.5 RBS's Information Security Issue

The article analyzed RBS's Information security issues. We selected the topic because it is a very important incident on IS. Information can be easily used to manipulate the victims and can cause serious problems. For the security of the information companies hire security companies to safely secure the information. But recently there was an incident regarding the Royal Bank of Scotland.

The bank suffered great loss because of the lack of the proper IS implementation. The customers of the bank were greatly hurt financially and the bank manager was disappointed with their IS implementation. The analysis has provided a detailed information on the incident and the authors have depicted the incident thoroughly and so the article was valid. And for that reason the article was chosen to be used to act as an example of internet security issue.

5.6 SAP Failure in California

This analysis discussed on incidents regarding IS implementation failure. It identifies IS implementation failure of a particular organization. MyCalPays is a software which was supposed to be designed but for some lack of information and other factors the software did not turn out to be what California hoped for. So they protested against the software and made a lawsuit against SAP. The loss of money was huge which is said to be an amount of 250 million. This huge money was wasted on the software. But SAP claimed that they had made no errors and the software did what was desired from it.

This huge loss of money created problems for both the parties and so the project was eventually dropped. The incident was greatly described by the author and the article was exact to the required example. The article was as a result valid.

Internet Connectivity

6.0 Optical Fibre and Related Issues

At present, Optical Fibre is the major medium of internet connectivity. The cables are contented the entire world and provide fast internet connectivity.

OPTICAL FIBER CONSTRUCTION

❑ **Core**
> Glass or plastic with a higher index of refraction than the cladding
> Carries the signal

❑ **Cladding**
> Glass or plastic with a lower index of refraction than the core

❑ **Buffer**
> Protects the fiber from damage and moisture

❑ **Jacket**
> Holds one or more fibers in a cable

Jacket
400 μm

Buffer
250 um

Cladding
125 μm

Core
8 μm

The optical fibres are a very important mode of data transferring but one of its major disadvantages is that it is very expensive. Though the price of these fibres has reduced in the last couple of years but it is still very costly despite of all these drop of prices.

Because of this high price range of this many broadband Internet Service providers are going out of business and it also creates a problem for the broadband users as it becomes more costly to set up the broadband connection for both in residence and also in corporate offices. And so we can learn from and know the graveness of damage of optical fibres.

6.1 Limitations Optical Fibre

This article tells us about the major impact on damage of optical fibre. This article is a common example of this happening and so it was taken. The optical fibre is such a special type of fibre made of glass which is used to carry electronic signals from one place to another. But this optical fibre has some limitation one of which is that this type of fibre is when bent may disrupt the inner glass materials and may even create a leakage.

This leakage can later on be taken advantage of by hacking information. This is though a critical process but still is possible to do which makes many information very open and vulnerable to hack. Not only that but also because of this inability to bend it can create problems of system loss. With this article we are informed about the impact on damage and limitation of optical fibre.

Recent Blackout Issues Regarding Optical Fibre

The fibre optic cable is a very important article because it is used to carry data from one place to another in a very little amount of time and also because it helps to provide internet supply too.

Recently, there has been a massive blackout of internet because of some faulty optical fibres which were mysteriously cut underwater. The result of this faulty submarine cables was no internet for many countries of the Middle East, Central & South Asia including countries like India, Saudi Arabia, and Egypt.

This outage took several days to fix and resulted in the blockage of 70% online traffic in Egypt and also cutting the bandwidth of India to 50-60%. This huge shutdown of internet because of the faulty optical fibre cable caused a great deal of loss to the banks and other institution of the affected countries.

6.2 GCI Company's Internet Outage

The optic fibres are a very necessary thing and that's why when it is damaged it can cause a lot of problems. In Alaska, a utility contractor cut through a big optical fibre cable which led to the internet outage for the users of GCI company. This outage caused a lot of problems because the place it was cut was found to be the connection point of about 550 fibre optic cables and this huge damage meant that they could not provide internet to their users for quite a longer period of time.

The damage was concluded to be very big for the company since it took a lot of time for them to be repaired and which obviously incurred them a heavy loss of money.

6.3 Damage of Fibre Optics through Massive Earthquake & Tsunami

This article shows the damage of undersea fibre optics due to massive earthquake and tsunami. I thought this would be helpful as a most obvious example of redundancy. It is true that redundancy is the common element of network design, but it can create a massive disruption. In 11/03/2011; 8.9 magnitude earthquake was taken place 231 miles northeast of Tokyo. After the earthquake a massive Tsunami was occurred in that area and killed thousands of people.

After that disaster, half of the existing fibre optic cables running under the Pacific were damaged. The fibre optic connection between US, Japan and Korea faced treble network disruption and internet based communication failure due to that earthquake under the sea. Pacific Crossing PC-1 W and PC-1 N parts of its network were out of service and this created fibre optic network failure in the pacific zone. The financial losses due to the damage of fibre optic cables were massive.

6.4 Typhoon Morakot Damaged the Undersea Fibre Optic Cables

This article shows how Typhoon Morakot damaged the undersea fibre optic cables. We chose this to show the real-life example of undersea fibre optic cables damage through natural disaster. The fibre optic cable can be damaged due to typhoon or cyclonic type's disasters. In August 2, 2009; Typhoon Morakot was swept past Taiwan and some other pacific countries.

Typhoon Morakot caused landslide under the sea that was the main reason behind this fibre optic cables damage. This was causing disruption to internet, online services and voice services in China and Southeast Asia. The service providing company Chunghwa was able to restore the backup systems and rerouting services by using the unaffected cables.

We found the internet connection between Twian, China and South Asia was disrupted after that massive typhoon. In September, 2009; Chunghwa was able to repair those six undersea fibre optic cables completely.

6.5 BT's Network Outage

The article disused on BT's network outages. We selected the article because the issue is highly problematic over the years and also takes a lot of hard work to fix. These problems create great sufferings to both the service providers and the customers. These types of issues can be impactful to both the parties' economic status. Recently, BT broadband service providers, who are known to be the biggest one in the world, faced network outage and this created a whole lot of problems for the company.

This network outage was devastating because of the great number of customers that BT has. It took them time for them to find out the source of outage and the customers were highly unhappy and disappointed about the incident.

So the given article is a very good example of this type of incidents and has also been nicely described by the author and very helpful too.

6.6 AWS Network Outage

The article analyzed AWS network outage issue. We selected the article because it is a major and recent internet problem. This has affected major companies and has also financially crippled some major companies too. One such event happened when Amazon web service in Sydney faced network outage. This was a very problematic situation because it took a long time for them to figure out the source of the outage and also the reason the outage took place. This problem created distress for their customers.

It was found that because of the outage of amazon the network of Domino's pizza and Foxtel Play and Foxtel Go also faced similar network outage but their problems were dealt with much sooner than that of amazon. The author nicely described the issue in his analysis. And for all these reasons this article is a good example of the incident

Social Networking of Corporate Giants

7.0 Powerful Social networking of Amazon

The article analyzed role of social networking for Amazon's business growth. This article was selected to identify world's major company's social networking processes.

Recently many major companies are trying hard to get involved in social networking to expand their business. One of these major companies is Amazon. Amazon have been trying very hard to expand their businesses with the help of social networking. Social networking of Amazon has been very active for the last couple of years. Amazon has always been active in both Facebook and twitter as much as they could.

Figure: An example of social networking strategy of Amazon

They have been able to implement their marketing strategy through social networking. They are also helping the customers and fixing their related issues. So it can be said that this article shows how Amazon has used social networking for their marketing purpose.

7.1 Apple's Strict Social Media Strategy

The analysis discussed on social networking system of Apple.

The topic was selected to identify Apple's social networking system. Apple is also major company in the world. It has been rocketing to the top for the last decades. The marketing system and strategy of the company has changed a bit with the introduction of social networking.

Apple do not have any endorsed Facebook or twitter pages but the pages of Apple store and Apple music do exist and are very famous in the social networks. The products of apple has created great benefits for apple because of the marketing strategy related to it and the fact that these products are famous in the social networking medias. The author has described the subject matter in the article thoroughly. And so it can be said that this article has been much useful.

Big data

8.0 Using Petabyte to Backup Big data

This article discusses about a technique about storing and backing up Big data. Moreover this article was chosen as it is an interesting technique on storing and backing up Big data. Big data is a set of enormously large data which can't be processed by traditional data application because of its huge amount of data.

One of its most challenging feature is its storage and backing it up. There is some possible solution to this problem;

one of these solution is to protect the petabytes. Petabytes are of a huge size and are often vulnerable so these data may be hampered unless it is backed up and stored carefully.

Figure: Big data Icons and Data Management Buttons

The most intelligent thing to do is to store the petabyte sized files or data according to preference and importance first. This technique can help us in storing and backing up Big data. The article shows the features of Petabyte to backup Big data, it is huge amount of data, that's hard to store or mange in a traditional data structure.

Thus, Big data needs different technologies to manage and store this enormous amount of data. Petabyte is huge amount data storing technology that can backup enormous amount Big data. It can also organize the data by following date and time structure.

The most necessary technique to backup the petabyte file type Big data according to initialize its importance and backup the file carefully. We have found the backup process is sometime vulnerable as the security system of petabyte isn't adequate, but as of now the technology is still working for backup and mange Big data.

8.1 Implementation of Hadoop as Big data Storage

A highly scalable analytics platform uses to process large volume of structured and unstructured data is Hadoop. Hadoop is an open source platform developed in 2005 and managed under Advance System Format (ASF), used as a concept of Mapreduce which is composed on two different functions. The Map step is a process where data is input and broken down for processing across nodes within a Hadoop instance.

For further processing, these "worker" nodes breaks the data down further. In the Reduced step, the processed data is then assembled back together into a format performing the original query. During the Map operation Hadoop's developers implemented a scale-out architecture based on many low-cost physical servers to cope with truly massive scale data analysis.

Their logic was to introduce a Hadoop system capable of faster processors, more memory and fast shared storage.

8.2 Backup Big data through Magnetic Tap

The article discusses on the importance Magnetic Tape to backup Big data. Although backup and organization process of Big data is always challenging, but we found some technologies can able to take this challenge. Another technique of backup and manage the Big data is Magnetic Tape. Big data having a huge amount of data to store and back up, it becomes a very big challenge to do so. And it maybe an even bigger problem if the technique for proper storage and back up is not known. There has been many techniques and suggestions for the storage of Big data and one of them is storage through magnetic tape. The magnetic tape offers more faster and cost effective data storage.

The statistics show that this method of backup and storage system meet the requirement of the users and also provides very good quality storage and backup. Enormous amount of Big data can be backup rapidly through the assistance of magnetic tape. This technology creates secured, user friendly environment for data management and backup. The technique is very cost effective and secured as well. And this technique can backup the Big data for a longer time period with a less vulnerability. And from this article we can learn how to store and back up Big data.

Thus, we have examined the system analyst are now preferring Magnetic Tape data backup system for Big data.

8.3 Storing Big data through Google Cloud Bigtable

Recently, Google has inaugurated a service for storing a huge amount of data online which in other words means Big data. Though it's new to the public but it was the service through which Google stored their files and data. The name of this service is Google Cloud Bigtable. Through this service people across multiple servers can store huge amount of data and also using the Application Programing Interface (API) service. People can read and write their data too with a much lower latency than normal. The customers can easily access the Bigtable using their software called Hadoop.

Moreover, the Bigtable offers its customers a more swift and secured way of storing Big data. Since Big data storing is a very hard task to manage these days Google has done an excellent work to open this service in the time of huge demands.

Success of Outsourcing

9.0 Success of Alibaba.com through Outsourcing

This article is about outsourcing success story of Alibaba.com. We selected it because it's a great success story of outsourcing. There are many major companies which were built upon successful outsourcing. Alibaba is one of the major company which was built on the basis of outsourcing.

It is a company inspired by the famous story "Alibaba & the Forty Thieves". The main moral taken from the story was that too much greed will destroy you but danger can be eliminated by forethought.

The company was built by 17 members who started doing outsourcing in China and because of the shortage of this type of service they speed to success in a small span of time. The given article has explained the story of Alibaba very nicely. And the author has been also able to bring out the major facts of their success too.

9.1 Slack Founder's Outsourcing Success

The analysis has been discussed Slack founder's runaway success. We chose it to identify the one of the great success story of outsourcing. People get opportunities to open their own business and other financial standings. There has been many cases where outsourcing has rocketed companies to top success and one of the cases was of Slack.

It is a company which was not supposed to be but it was a very small company making apps and similar things. It was helped by metlab to make their apps designs and soon with some major apps sale Slack flew to the gateway of success. Many other companies have tried the same strategy but have not gone close to the success of Slack. The given article provides a good idea about the success of Slack and the author was successful to point out the reasons too.

Chronology of Outsourcing Disasters

10.0 IBM's Outsourcing Failure

This article discusses about a major outsourcing failure. This article was chosen as it was a famous incident on the given topic. Outsourcing is not a very easy medium for livelihood. It may have some serious outcomes when any organizations fail to meet the requirements. It may even be so grave that it may put an organization out of the business. One of the greatest outsourcing disaster happened when IBM failed in their deal with Austin energy which went horribly wrong for them.

The reason was many deadlines which were missed and software's full of bugs and also the same types of errors were made repeatedly and some key tasks were not done in time. And for these faulty errors resulted in an overall huge failure. This failure is a big disappointment for IBM for their stature and class.

The company faced another outsourcing failure recently. IBM was initialized with a contract with Queensland to develop an application to administrate payroll for Queensland's health department in December 2007. By mid-2008, for $6 million, IBM proposed to complete the project. After beginning the project IBM shortly realized that the project will face numerous and a number of unforeseen technical challenges and claimed to Queensland that the project would cost $27 million. Like this, the project went on for some years but the payroll never functioned properly.

And in the interim, thousands of staff failed to receive the pay checks while some others were over paid. In the end, the cost of the project escalated to $1.2 billion which is 16,000 per cent above the projected cost. Then IBM was banned from working on any government project by Queensland and was sued to recover its losses. Queensland learned that not ever famous-name vendor earns famous results. This article helps us to watch out for two major outsourcing failures of IBM.

10.1 Royal Bank's Outsourcing Failure

The article shows the example failure of outsourcing at Royal Bank of Scotland in 2012. We chose it to show the famous example failure of outsourcing. The bank outsourced their banking software from a popular software company. The software cloud process incoming and outgoing transactions, it could also process the transaction history of the account holders.

But once the software failed to process the overnight transfers and transaction history of the account holders that caused a serious problem for both account holders and the bank. Because the customers were unable to withdraw, transfer or view their accounts detail. In the meantime, the bank also failed to conduct the transfers of the commercial customers. It is reported that, 30,000 social welfare recipient couldn't receive their payments, even though their funds were transferred from the govt. account.

We found, this failure not only affected the RBS account holders but also affected British bank NatWest and Ireland's Ulster Bank account holders.

It is reported that the Bank faced another outsourcing failure in 2008. In the autumn of 2008, the debacle that happened to the Royal Bank of Scotland (RBS) is as serious as it can get for any bank. It is the responsibility of every bank to let their customers execute transactions and see what funds they have available. But if any problem occurs and if not dealt seriously then it can impact on the bank's viability.

Some other major outsourcing and technological failures have been seen in the UK's banking industry. Back in 14 September 2007, technological failure was seen in Northern Rock (A British Bank) and their customers were not being able to access into their online account on 13 September and then the bank was disclosed and was handed to the Bank of England for emergency funding. And they were short of server capacity to know what was actually going on. After that, all Banks have been requested to increase their server capacity so that they can handle online traffic equivalent to 300% of normal demand.

10.2 Virgin Blue Airlines Outsourcing Failure

The article is on the information of an outsourcing failure. This article was worth choosing because it created great damage and is a renowned incident.

The virgin blue airlines were the victim of an IT failure when their booking system glitches and this resulted the delay for the flights of people counting at least of 50,000.

The main reason for this IT disaster was because of a crashed hardware and for which they had to switch it to manual and this resulted in the delay of flights. This problem took a more grave side as the problem was failed to be dealt with in the required amount of time. Though it was later on fixed, the problem did last for longer time as it had to resolve its back logged flights. And so from this article we can learn from this mishaps and be cautious when needed.

10.3 Outsourcing Failure in US Navy

The article discusses on another outsourcing failure, that was happened between IT contractor Electronic Data Systems (EDS) and the US Navy. We selected it to show another serious failure of outsourcing. This was happened due to breakdown in communication between EDS and US navy that led to a major outsource disaster.

In 2000, US Navy and Marine Corps contracted EDS to deliver voice, video, network, desktops, laptop and system training for their personnel. EDS didn't analyze the overall agreements. For that reason, it faced major breakdown and lost over $500 million dollars assets.

This complex contractual agreement forced EDS to provide all kinds of hardware, software and legacy software related supports for US navy.

A silly communication breakdown caused the loss of $153 million dollars as well. We have analyzed these massive losses of outsourcing through this discussion.

References

Barraclough, C. (2015). *What is iOS and what does iOS stand for?*. [online] Recombu. Available at: https://recombu.com/mobile/article/what-is-ios-and-what-does-ios-stand-for [Accessed 12 May 2016]

Computer Article, (2015). *Different RAM Types and its uses*. [online] Computermemoryupgrade.net. Available at: http://www.computermemoryupgrade.net/types-of-computer-memory-common-uses.html [Accessed 26 Sep. 2016].

excITingIP.com. (2010). *Advantages and limitations of optical fiber Cable/ Communication*. [online] Available at: http://www.excitingip.com/978/advantages-and-disadvantages-of-ofc-optical-fiber-cable-communication/ [Accessed 12 May 2016].

Hub Tech Insider. (2009). *The advantages and disadvantages of fiber optics*. [online] Available at: https://hubtechinsider.wordpress.com/2009/06/04/the-advantages-and-disadvantages-of-fiber-optics/ [Accessed 10 May 2016].

Inquirer, T. (2016). *Google: five problems that need to be addressed to avoid killer AI invasion | TheINQUIRER*.

Intel. (2016). *Serial ATA (SATA)*. [online] Available at: http://www.intel.com/content/www/us/en/io/serial-ata/serial-ata-developer.html [Accessed 21 May 2016].

Informationweek. (2016). *Chronology Of an outsourcing disaster - informationweek*. [online] Available at: http://www.informationweek.com/it-strategy/chronology-of-an-outsourcing-disaster/d/d-id/1102987? [Accessed 12 May 2016].

Information-age.com. (2016). *Australian airline grounded by IT failure | Information Age*. [online] Available at: http://www.information-age.com/it-management/outsourcing-and-supplier-management/1286558/australian-airline-grounded-by-it-failure [Accessed 14 May 2016].

James, J. (2010). *Microsoft's azure cloud computing platform: An overview for developers - TechRepublic*. [online] TechRepublic. Available at: http://www.techrepublic.com/blog/software-engineer/microsofts-azure-cloud-computing-platform-an-overview-for-developers/ [Accessed 10 May 2016].

Linktionary.com. (2016). *SCSI (Small Computer System Interface) (Linktionary term)*. [online] Available at: http://www.linktionary.com/s/scsi.html [Accessed 20 May 2016].

Mountain, I. (2016). *The History of Magnetic Tape and Computing: A 65-Year-Old Marriage Continues to Evolve*. [online] Ironmountain.com.

O'Keeffe, (2013). *Embedded Linux Debugging Techniques An Overview*. [online] Available at: http://www.ashling.com/wp-content/uploads/EmbeddedLinuxDebuggingOverview.pdf [Accessed 27 Sep. 2016].

PCMAG. (2016). *IDrive*. [online] Available at: http://www.pcmag.com/article2/0,2817,2362675,00.asp [Accessed 25 May 2016].

Perl Maven. (2016). *What is Unicode*. [online] Available at: http://perlmaven.com/unicode [Accessed 13 May 2016]. Tech-faq.com. (2015). *EBCDIC (Extended Binary Coded Decimal Interchange Code)*. [online] Available at: http://www.tech-faq.com/ebcdic.html [Accessed 25 May 2016].

Qnx, (2014). *What is QNX Momentics?*. [online] Qnx.de. Available at:http://www.qnx.de/developers/docs/6.4.0/momentics/welcome/whatis.html [Accessed 25 Sep. 2016].

Research.ibm.com. (2016). *IBM research - Zurich: Cloud & computing infrastructure, storage techniques for Big data*. [online] Available at: https://www.research.ibm.com/labs/zurich/sto/bigdata.html [Accessed 10 May 2016].

SearchCloudComputing. (2016). *What is Engine Yard? - Definition from WhatIs.com*. [online] Available at: http://searchcloudcomputing.techtarget.com/definition/Engine-Yard [Accessed 11 May 2016].

SearchSecurity. (2016). *What is phishing? - Definition from WhatIs.com*. [online] Available at: http://searchsecurity.techtarget.com/definition/phishing [Accessed 14 May 2016].

SearchCIO. (2016). *What is pretexting? - Definition from whatis.com*. [online] Available at: http://searchcio.techtarget.com/definition/pretexting [Accessed 11 May 2016].

SearchDataBackup. (2016). *Protecting petabytes: Best practices for Big data backup*. [online] Available at: http://searchdatabackup.techtarget.com/feature/Protecting-petabytes-Best-practices-for-big-data-backup [Accessed 10 May 2016].

Silverthorne, (2015). *A closer look at the Amazon Web Services cloud platform*. [online] Search Cloud Computing. Available at: http://searchcloudcomputing.techtarget.com/feature/A-closer-look-at-the-Amazon-Web-Services-cloud-platform [Accessed 26 Sep. 2016].

Todd, A. and Barraclough, C. (2016). *What is android and what is an android phone?*. [online] Recombu. Available at: https://recombu.com/mobile/article/what-is-android-and-what-is-an-android-phone_M12615.html [Accessed 11 May 2016].

TopTenREVIEWS. (2016). *Dropbox cloud services review 2016 - Top Ten Reviews*. [online] Available at: http://cloud-services-review.toptenreviews.com/dropbox-review.html [Accessed 11 May 2016].

About the Author

Ghazi Mokammel Hossain is a professional e-book, article, research, analysis paper and a creative writer. He has written some books as well as many articles, research papers, analysis and creative articles. The author is also a freelance writer as well as a researcher. He was born on 31 December, 1993. He has passed his S.S.C exam from Dhaka under Dhaka Board in 2008 and passed his H.S.C exam from Dhaka under Dhaka Board in 2010. He has graduated with a Bachelor's of Business Administration in HRM in 2015 from a renowned University. He has also completed Computer Science and Engineering certificate course in 2011.

He published his first book called "IPv4 IP6 Technology & Implementation" in Amazon Kindle and Createspace on 2013. The author published his second book called "Introduction to Network on Chip Routing Algorithms" in 2014. He also published "Fundamental of API Based Financial Engineering" and "Ebola Epidemic: A Detail Survival Guide From Ebola Virus Disease Outbreak" in 2014. The author published an outstanding thrilling novel called "Anwar: Emergence of Unknown Defenders" in 2016 on Amazon kindle and Createspace. Playing football, Cricket, PC games, reading books, novel, research paper, cycling and mountain climbing are his favorite hobbies.

Also By Ghazi Mokammel Hossain & GM Publishers

ICT World: Development, Failure of Computer & Smartphone Technologies- November, 2016 by Ghazi Mokammel Hossain, Md. Fazle Mubin, Md. Izhar Tahmid, & Md. Fathe Mubin

Supermarket Management Practices: In the Changing Economic Environment- November, 2016 by Ghazi Mokammel Hossain

https://www.amazon.com/dp/B01MFGHM6X

Anwar: Emergence of Unknown Defenders- August 10, 2016 by Ghazi Mokammel Hossain

https://www.amazon.com/dp/B01K8KLIJ8

The Survival of USA – Part Two: A Novel - August, 2016 by Ghazi Mokammel Hossain & MD. Fazle Mubin

https://www.amazon.com/dp/B01K8I4Z0E

Business Environment: Theoretical & Organizational Aspects – July, 2016 by Ghazi Mokammel Hossain

https://www.amazon.com/dp/B01HTQYG7A

The Survival of USA - Part One: A Novel – March, 2016 by Ghazi Mokammel Hossain, MD. Fazle Mubin & Pranjal Rahman

https://www.amazon.com/dp/B01CTXNF8E

Enterprise IPv6 for Enterprise Networks- December, 2015 by Ghazi Mokammel Hossain & Fathe Mubin

https://www.amazon.com/dp/B017U84ISO

Heart of Democracy: A Versatile Poetry Book - Aug 28, 2015 by Ghazi Mozammel Hossain

https://www.amazon.com/dp/B014MTHGRY

The Brave Parrot of Jungle - Dec 11, 2014 by Syeda Taskin Ara & Gulshan Ahmed

https://www.amazon.com/dp/B00QXHW4PS

IPv4 IPv6 Technology and Implementation - Nov 2, 2013 by Ghazi Mokammel Hossain & GM Hossain

https://www.amazon.com/dp/B00GEHNC8K

The Mirror of Religion - Jul 19, 2015 by Ghazi Mozammel Hossain & Richard Marks

https://www.amazon.com/dp/B01204ROIO

Introduction to Network on Chip Routing Algorithms - Oct 4, 2014 by Ghazi Mokammel Hossain

https://www.amazon.com/dp/B00O6ET3J0

Ebola Epidemic: A Detail Survival Guide From Ebola Virus Disease Outbreak - Oct 25, 2014 by Ghazi Mokammel Hossain & Dr. Robert Alex

https://www.amazon.com/dp/B00OWG4TL4

Fundamental of API Based Financial Engineering - Oct 17, 2014 by Ghazi Mokammel Hossain

https://www.amazon.com/dp/B00OJJJJO6

For more details please visit Amazon Author Central
https://www.amazon.com/Ghazi-Mokammel-Hossain/e/B00GGATR2K/ref=dp_byline_cont_ebooks_1

GM Publishers
My Book My Life

www.ingramcontent.com/pod-product-compliance
Lightning Source LLC
Chambersburg PA
CBHW070858070326
40690CB00009B/1893